INKUBATOR

ADRIANA LUNA CARLOS
Editor-In-Chief, Designer
and Co-Founder

HANNA OLIVAS
Managing Editor &
Co-Founder

ADVERTISING OPPORTUNITIES

Info@SheRisesStudios.com

INKUBATOR MAGAZINE
JULY 2025

SHE RISES
STUDIOS

CONTACT US

SheRisesStudios@gmail.com

WWW.SHERISESSTUDIOS.COM

LETTER FROM THE EDITORS

Dear Readers,

Welcome to the July 2025 edition of Inkubator Magazine, where bold voices rise and fearless stories find their wings.

This month, we proudly present our theme: "Write Outside the Lines: Bold Stories, Fearless Voices, Limitless Pages"—a tribute to the women who are rewriting the narrative, refusing to be boxed in, and daring to lead with purpose and power.

Our cover feature, Christine Davis, is a shining embodiment of that boldness. A nurse, author, entrepreneur, and creative force, Christine brings peace, healing, and empowerment to every page she touches. From coloring books that restore the soul to community initiatives that uplift others, her story reminds us that even in life's darkest chapters, there is always light to be written in.

We also spotlight the Her Bold Steps Summit, aired exclusively on FENIX TV, where women stepped into their power and took the stage to share stories that shake ceilings and spark change. Inside this issue, you'll meet a dynamic lineup of authors, speakers, and creators who are fearlessly leading with their pens—and their presence.

At Inkubator, we believe that every voice matters. Whether you're penning your first paragraph or publishing your fifth book, this space is for you. Let these stories stir your passion, reignite your creativity, and remind you that the power to impact lives starts with one brave sentence.

Here's to writing without limits—and living the story only you can tell.

Warm regards,

Adriana Luna Carlos & Hanna Olivas
Editors of Inkubator Magazine

COLORING THROUGH GRIEF, HEALING WITH FAITH:

The Transformational Journey of **Christine Davis**

In a world often marked by chaos and uncertainty, Christine Davis offers a calming presence and a message of hope. A nurse, entrepreneur, author, and community leader, Christine's multifaceted journey is deeply rooted in faith, creativity, and resilience. Through her inspired projects—especially her bestselling coloring books and empowering journals—she is helping countless women discover inner peace, embrace their true identities, and cultivate wholeness in mind, body, and spirit.

Christine's first coloring book, Color with the Word: 60 Days of Peace and Color, began as a quiet whisper in her heart—a gentle urge to create something that could bring calm to others amid life's storms. The concept was simple yet profound: combining scripture with creative expression to foster moments of peace. However, Christine admits she wasn't sure how her work would be received or even if it would come to fruition.

It wasn't until she experienced a deeply personal loss that the true purpose of the book became clear. After the passing of her father, Christine found herself engulfed in grief. One day, her daughter invited her to color together. Initially hesitant, Christine finally agreed after several gentle requests. What unfolded in that quiet time surprised her—she felt a soothing calm that momentarily lifted the heaviness in her heart. That small act of coloring sparked a healing shift that transcended words.

"That moment changed everything," Christine reflects. *"I knew I had to finish this book—not just for me, but for every person seeking stillness in the chaos of life."*

Since its release, Color with the Word has resonated with readers far beyond what Christine ever imagined. Women share how the book helps them reflect, pray, and reconnect with their inner peace one page at a time. It's not merely a coloring book—it's a gentle journey toward wholeness.

Christine's academic background is as diverse as her creative pursuits. Holding degrees in nursing, biology, and business, she credits these disciplines for shaping her entrepreneurial approach. Nursing taught her empathy and how to truly care for people, skills that remain foundational to her work. Biology sharpened her analytical and problem-solving abilities, while business studies equipped her with the tools to build sustainable systems.

Together, these fields have helped Christine become a well-rounded entrepreneur who leads with both heart and insight. *"My education has allowed me to balance compassion with strategy,"* she explains. *"That balance is essential when you're creating meaningful work and running a business."*

For nearly 20 years, Christine has worked as a virtual specialist while raising her family—a balancing act she describes as an ongoing practice of presence and grace. *"Balance isn't about doing everything at once; it's about being fully present in each moment,"* she shares. Setting boundaries, prioritizing what matters most, and allowing herself to evolve without chasing perfection are her guiding principles.

Her creative projects and community involvement are natural extensions of who she is, integrated thoughtfully alongside her family and career. This approach allows her to nurture both personal fulfillment and professional growth simultaneously.

Beyond her coloring books, Christine authored a journal called I AM, designed to help women rediscover their identity in God beyond their roles as mothers, wives, or caretakers. *"Being a mother or wife is a divine gift,"* Christine says, *"but it's not the whole story. There is so much more inside us—dreams, callings, and capabilities waiting to be embraced."*

Her co-authored coloring book with Jeremy Green, born from shared grief after losing their loved ones, offers another layer of healing. After Christine lost her mother and then, just a week later, her husband unexpectedly passed away, she and Jeremy found solace in turning their pain into a resource for others navigating loss. This book supports those grieving not only death but also other forms of loss—jobs, relationships, or a sense of self.

Christine hopes women understand grief as layered and personal, but also that creative outlets can provide peace and clarity when words fail. *"Art holds space for healing,"* she says. *"You are not alone, and there is rest even in pain."*

Christine's heartfelt work has not gone unnoticed. Featured in influential publications such as Success Savvy Magazine and Million Dollar Mom Society Magazine, she views these honors as affirmations that her voice and story matter. *"Being recognized is humbling and motivates me to keep creating space for others to rise,"* she explains.

She was also honored as a role model for Model US, a title she holds dear for its affirmation of authenticity, faith, and integrity. Professionally and personally, it reflects the impact she aspires to have—especially for young women searching for strength beyond the spotlight. *"Being a role model means showing up fully, even when the platform isn't what you expected,"* Christine says.

At the EmpowerHER Virtual Summit, Christine delivered a message titled Peaceful Prosperity, inviting women to redefine prosperity beyond financial wealth. For her, true prosperity encompasses mental well-being, emotional stability, spiritual growth, and meaningful relationships.

"When we cultivate peace in one area, it ripples into abundance in others," she explained to the audience. Christine encouraged women to see peace not as absence of struggle but presence of clarity, purpose, and faith—a balanced life where peace and prosperity fuel each other.

Christine understands the challenges women entrepreneurs face, especially self-doubt and burnout. Her advice? *"Remember why you started, but give yourself permission to pause."* She encourages building supportive networks, celebrating small wins, and embracing growth at your own pace.

"Protect your peace fiercely," she stresses. *"Whether it's coloring, journaling, or quiet reflection, hold onto what grounds you. Remove anything or anyone that consistently robs your peace.*

Walk in grace but with confidence—God is a God of clarity and purpose, not confusion."

Christine's passion for connection extends beyond her books. She is actively involved with organizations like Jackson Woman for Good and the Worldwide Women's Association, where she finds inspiration among purpose-driven women committed to leadership and service.

As Managing Partner of the She Wins Women's Network in Jackson, Mississippi, Christine is spearheading a local networking event aimed at empowering women in mental wellness, entrepreneurship, spiritual clarity, and holistic growth. Whether through her published works, public speaking, or community outreach, Christine Davis continues to plant seeds of healing and hope—one heart, one story, one act of faith at a time.

Connect With Christine

www.anointedassistant.com

FENIX TV

YOUR PLATFORM, YOUR VOICE, YOUR POWER!

STEP INTO THE SPOTLIGHT AS A HOST ON FENIX TV!

Are you ready to amplify your message, inspire others, and be part of a groundbreaking network dedicated to empowering women worldwide? FENIX TV is your platform to shine as a host, share your expertise, and connect with a global audience.

WHY HOST ON FENIX TV?

- Reach a worldwide audience passionate about empowerment
- Showcase your voice, brand, and expertise
- Join a community of inspiring leaders and changemakers
- Be part of a network that uplifts and celebrates women

Whether you dream of leading a talk show, sharing powerful stories, or educating and inspiring others—FENIX TV is where your voice matters!

SECURE YOUR SPOT TODAY!

 Contact us now at
info@fenixtv.app

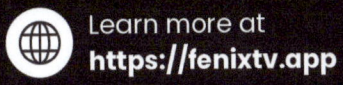 Learn more at
https://fenixtv.app

COURAGEOUS WOMAN:

Carmen Maendel's Journey to Wellness, Faith, and Inner Strength

What does it take to become truly unstoppable? Not just physically strong, but emotionally resilient, spiritually grounded, and empowered to rise from life's toughest moments? For Carmen Maendel, the answer lies in one powerful truth: Your health is your wealth—and when you cast your cares upon Jesus, you find the courage to rise.

Featured in the powerful anthology Becoming an Unstoppable Woman in Health & Wellness, Carmen's story, Courageous Woman: Casting Cares Upon Jesus, is a testament to what happens when faith meets fierce determination. This isn't just a chapter—it's a call to arms for any woman who's ever battled stress, burnout, or self-doubt and needed a way to come back stronger, healthier, and more aligned with her purpose.

From Struggle to Strength

Like many of the authors in this compilation, Carmen shares more than wellness tips—she shares lived experience. Her journey is steeped in the challenges so many women face: mental exhaustion, spiritual fatigue, and the disconnection between body, mind, and soul. But instead of staying stuck, Carmen chose faith. She chose healing. She chose herself.

Her message is clear: when we surrender our burdens and trust God with the process, we unlock a deeper strength. Through practical strategies and spiritual insight, Carmen helps women understand how to re-center their lives, care for their bodies, and cultivate the confidence to move forward.

A Health-First, Faith-Fueled Blueprint

In this powerful collection created by She Rises Studios' founders Hanna Olivas and Adriana Luna Carlos, Carmen's voice shines as one of deep authenticity and unwavering encouragement. Alongside 30+ other unstoppable women, she explores how healing doesn't start with grand gestures—it starts with small, intentional choices made from a place of love and belief.

Whether it's prioritizing self-care, learning to listen to your body, or developing a resilient, health-positive mindset, Courageous Woman offers practical wisdom grounded in real-life transformation. Carmen weaves her faith throughout her story, reminding readers that holistic wellness is as much about our spiritual posture as it is about nutrition or fitness routines.

When Women Rise, the World Changes

Becoming an Unstoppable Woman in Health & Wellness is more than a book—it's a movement. Founded by mother-daughter duo Hanna Olivas and Adriana Luna Carlos, She Rises Studios has become a global force for women's empowerment. The anthology celebrates the intersection of personal health, empowerment, and purpose, proving that when women invest in themselves, they invest in generations to come.

Carmen's story embodies this mission. She doesn't just talk about health—she models it through courage, consistency, and compassion. Her chapter is a warm, faith-based invitation to every woman who feels overwhelmed or overlooked: you are not alone, and you are never too far gone to start again.

The Courage to Care—for You

As we celebrate voices that dare to write outside the lines in this premiere issue of Inkubator Magazine, Carmen Maendel reminds us that sometimes the boldest stories come from the quiet moments of surrender. From the whispered prayers to the hard decisions, to the steady rebuilding of a life rooted in strength and grace.

Courageous Woman is for every woman ready to stop surviving and start thriving. It's for the woman looking in the mirror and deciding to honor herself—not just in body, but in spirit.

www.sherisesstudios.com

COURAGE
Woman
Casting Cares Upon J

CARMEN K. MAE

COURAGEOUS
Woman
Casting Cares Upon Jesus

CARMEN K. MAENDEL

WHAT THE FUNK?!

Molly Smith's Bold Wake-Up Call to Women Everywhere

Let's be honest—who among us hasn't hit that point where everything just feels... off? Where your spark has dimmed, your energy is drained, and the life you're living feels miles away from the one you dreamed of? If you've ever found yourself staring in the mirror and wondering, "What the funk is going on with my life?"—then Molly Smith wrote this book for you.

In What the Funk?!: A Practical Guide to Getting Out of the Funk You Are In With Your Health, Mindset & Purpose, Smith delivers more than just a pep talk—she hands readers a mirror, a map, and a megaphone. This is not your typical self-help book with fluffy mantras and vague advice. It's a raw, honest, and empowering guide for women who are tired of going through the motions and ready to reclaim their power.

From Funk to Fulfillment

Molly Smith knows funk—she's lived it. Her approach is grounded in real-life experience, not theory. Through candid storytelling and practical wisdom, she invites readers into her world of transformation, showing exactly how she went from being stuck in fear and self-doubt to living in alignment with her health, passion, and purpose. And more importantly, she shows you how to do the same.

What sets this book apart is its refreshing honesty. Molly doesn't sugarcoat the discomfort that comes with growth, nor does she pretend change happens overnight. Instead, she champions the power of small, intentional steps. From shifting your mindset to aligning your priorities, What the Funk?! offers a roadmap to help you get real, get clear, and get moving.

Real Talk, Real Tools

At the heart of the book is Molly's deep belief that feeling off-track isn't a sign of failure—it's a wake-up call. And with the right tools and mindset, that wake-up call can become a launchpad.

She guides you to pinpoint exactly what's out of sync—be it your health, your relationships, or your sense of purpose—and then gently nudges you toward clarity and momentum.

Each chapter feels like a conversation with a wise, no-BS best friend who's been there. There's humor, heart, and hard truths—alongside actionable strategies to move from stuck to thriving. Readers will find themselves nodding along, laughing, maybe crying, and most importantly, finally feeling seen.

A Voice That Writes Outside the Lines

Molly Smith isn't interested in playing it safe. In a world that often tells women to stay quiet, stay small, or stay comfortable, her voice dares to say otherwise. What the Funk?! belongs in this premiere issue of Inkubator Magazine because it embodies everything we're celebrating—bold storytelling, fearless truth-telling, and the courage to break the mold.

This book doesn't just inspire change; it initiates it. It's for the woman who's tired of faking fine, who's ready to stop spinning her wheels, and who's willing to take that first brave step toward something better.

Ready to Get Out of Your Funk?

If you're craving a life that feels more aligned, more energized, and more you, then What the Funk?! might be the book that changes everything. Molly Smith isn't promising perfection—she's offering possibility. And in a world that needs more real, raw, and resilient voices, hers is one that echoes long after the last page.

So go ahead—turn the page, take the leap, and ask yourself: What the funk are you waiting for?

www.sherisesstudios.com

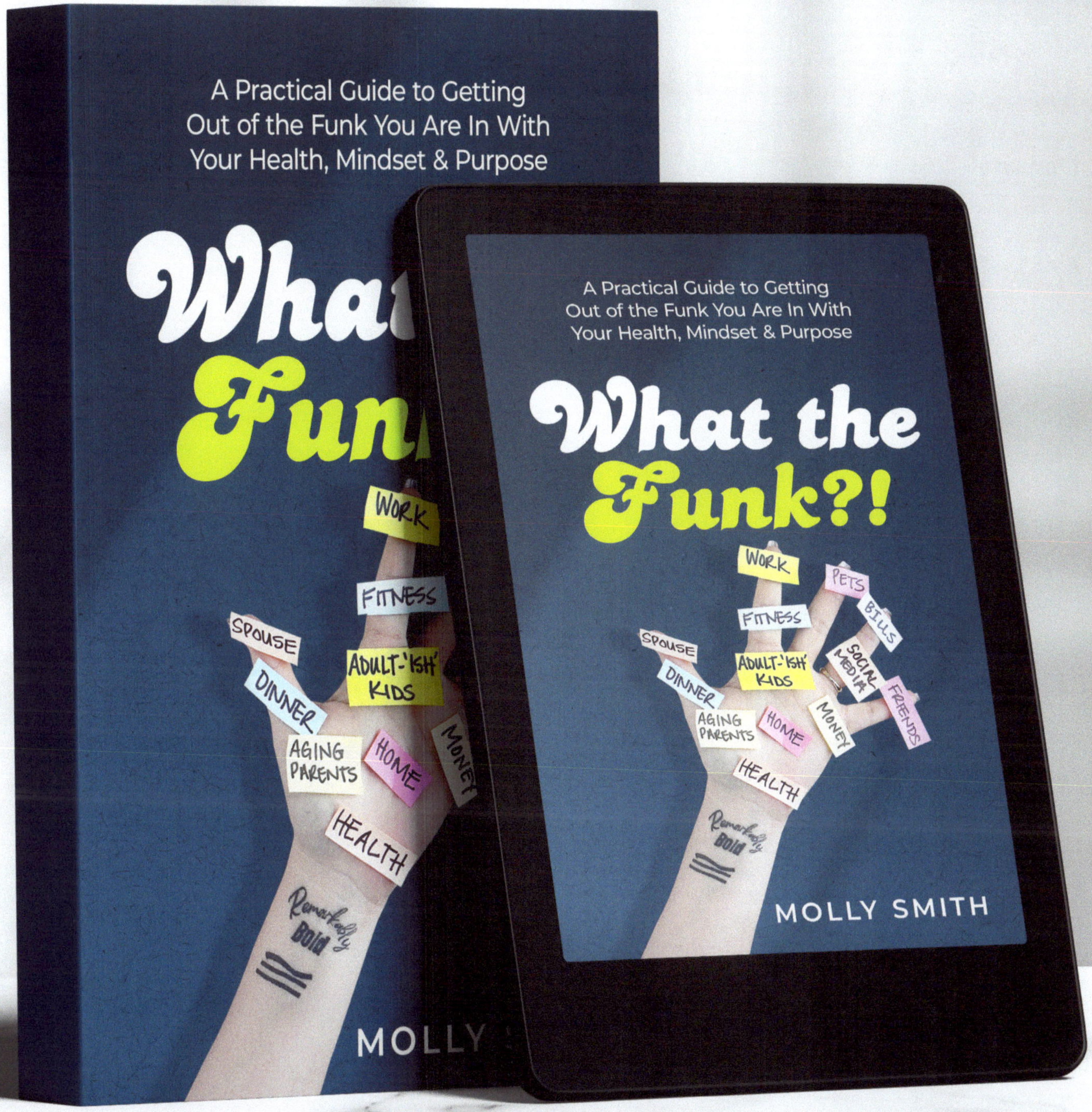
A Practical Guide to Getting
Out of the Funk You Are In With
Your Health, Mindset & Purpose
What the
Funk?!
WORK
PETS
BILLS
FITNESS
SPOUSE
ADULT-'ISH' KIDS
SOCIAL MEDIA
DINNER
FRIENDS
AGING PARENTS
HOME
MONEY
HEALTH
Remarkably Bold
MOLLY SMITH

The SHE RISES STUDIOS PODCAST

TUNE IN. RISE UP. THRIVE.

Looking for **real conversations** that inspire, empower, and ignite your potential? The **SRS Podcast** is where women like you come to **learn, grow, and rise!**

Join us for powerful **interviews with trailblazing entrepreneurs, thought leaders, and everyday women** who have turned obstacles into opportunities. Our episodes dive into:

➤ **Breaking through self-doubt** and stepping into confidence
➤ **Building a thriving business** with purpose and passion
➤ **Mastering work-life balance** without guilt
➤ **Leveling up your mindset, health, and career**
➤ **Finding your true purpose and living boldly**

Each episode is packed with **real stories, expert insights, and actionable strategies** to help you take your life to the next level. **This isn't just a podcast—it's your roadmap to success!**

SUBSCRIBE NOW AND START YOUR JOURNEY TO EMPOWERMENT!

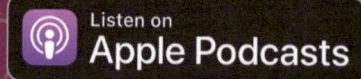

HELENKAGAN
HEALINGARTS™

By Helen Kagan PhD

Helen Kagan PhD, a scientist, psychologist, holistic therapist, artist, is a creator of her unique concept HealingArts™ of 30 years integrating Art of Healing, Expressive Arts & Fine Art. Her mission-driven purpose is to bring HealingArts™ to HealthCare, Residential & Hospitality Markets to assist in recovery & wellness, enhance healing & wellbeing.

HealingArts™ is exhibited in multiple venues, national & International Shows, Artsy.net, major ArtFairs (ArtExpo, ArtBasel, RedDot, Spectrum), named "Collectible Artist" by many sources, published, awarded, podcasted, filmed, and begins her own TalkShow with BoldBrave TV. Helen's work is simultaneously transformational, introspective, vibrant, multidimensional, and healing. A first-generation Russian-American, she brings her unique point-of-view conveying the seriousness of the current real and alternate aka *"new normal"* times, and a sensitive Soul, not foreign to the colorful abstraction of the modern Russian artistic tradition.

Bestselling Author, an *"Inspiring Woman-Leader"* by several International Magazines with Cover features,

a Jewish refugee from a former USSR, a pioneer in intentionally creating art for healing, Dr. Kagan continues to create her unique art for healing individuals and society.

Helen is also developing her new unique colorful creation - Wearable HealingArts® with each designer item made from her own HealingArts™ where art and healing unite in beautifully crafted, high-energy garments, and is looking for partners and sponsors in Interior & Fashion Design, HealthCare & Hospitality.

In her own words:
"My mission & purpose is to encourage healing through art. In our turbulent times, amid World-wide crises, wars, fear, anxiety, stress, overwhelm & uncertainty I feel it's my duty to continue create art for healing. A severe complex PTSD survivor dedicated my life helping others, a pioneer in intentional creating art for healing, I believe in mind-body-spirit & art as a catalyst for healing individuals society & environment. I believe that now, more than ever, our World needs positive energy, spiritual intentions, gratitude, and lots of positive healing art!

Art Investment & Collectors' Guide 2025:

· MOST INVESTABLE & PROMINENT ARTISTS ·

Helen Kagan HeaingArts Third Eye - My Universe. Series Healing Chakras. 2015-18. Acrylic on canvas 122x122cm

My passionate vibrant HealingArts called symphony of color and a vehicle for joy and well-being, is a statement of all my beliefs."

"Creating Harmony". Series Kintsugi.
Acrylic on canvas 48"x36"

This unique artwork embodies the philosophy of finding beauty in imperfection and healing through art. It is inspired by the traditional Japanese practice of Kintsugi - the mending of broken pottery with gold. My *"Kintsugi"* painting employs abstract forms, the whole spectrum of healing colors, textured surfaces, and gold-accented fissures to mimic the traditional Kintsugi technique, transforming perceived imperfections into focal points of beauty, meaning and healing.

Echoing the abstract expressionist approach, composition resists literal representation, instead allowing emotion, and symbolism to drive the viewer's experience. The use of layered paint and mixed mediums creates a tactile surface to activate your senses, while reinforcing the idea that harmony is forged not through uniformity, but through the integration of beauty, spirit, loss, and repair/healing into a cohesive, elevated whole.

Through deliberate fractures rendered in the composition and shimmering gold-like accents tracing these breaks, the painting communicates a powerful narrative of resilience, transformation, and unity. Soft, harmonious colors blend with graceful golden lines to evoke emotional depth, suggesting that harmony is not the absence of flaws, but the integration of them into a stronger, more meaningful powerful whole. The work invites viewers to reconsider the value of damage and healing, turning what was once broken into a testament of strength, beauty, and aesthetic grace.

Connect With Helen

www.HelenKagan.com
www.HelenKagan.net
www.WearableHealingArts.com
www.facebook.com/helenkagan
www.instagram.com/helenkaganarts
www.linkedin.com/in/healer

WRITING MY WAY FORWARD:

From Dream to Purpose

By Lisa Jacovsky

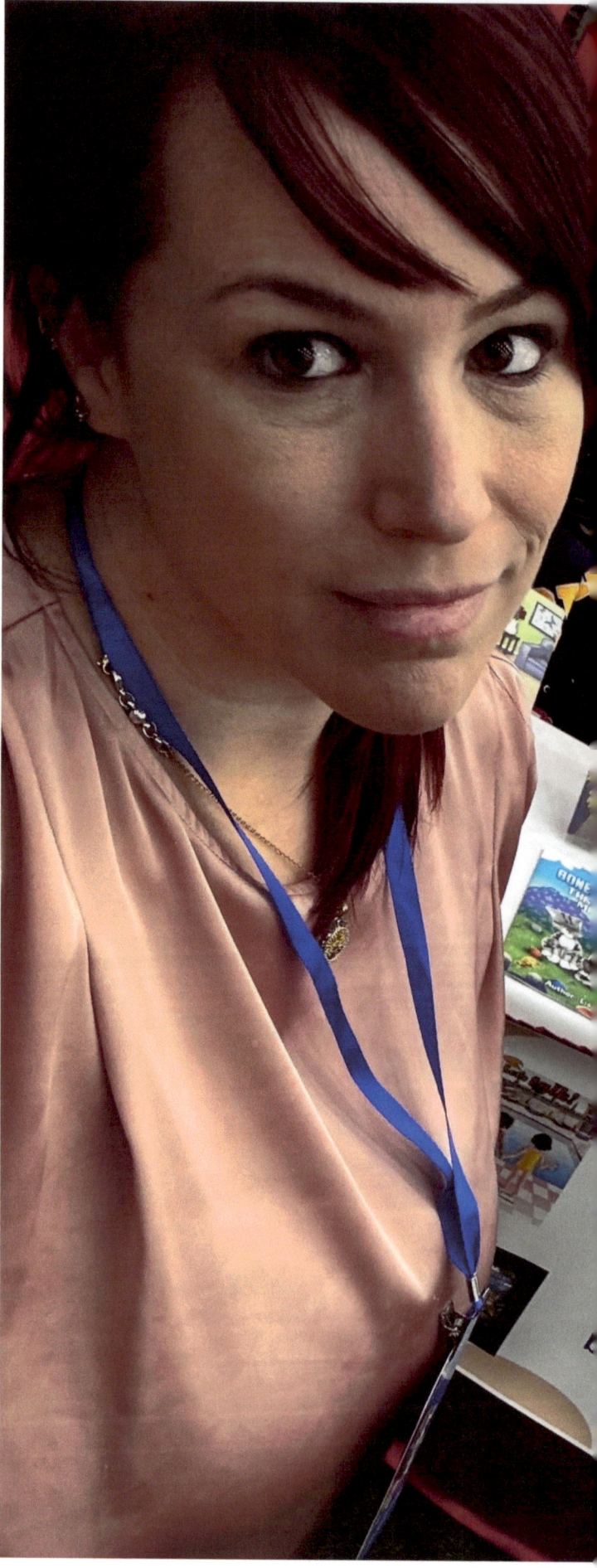

What started as something to reflect my career and experiences in the field of psychology, to show the world a different, more positive view of autism, has become something so much more. I started with one book in the hopes that one person would read it and become more accepting. I never expected my writing to connect to so many people.

I knew in writing my first book that I could receive pushback or even negative reviews. This could be because it had the word autism in the title, and possibly due to the subject. I never once doubted that title or thought about changing any part of my book. Neither did my support system, who always encouraged me. After numerous rejections from traditional publishers, I pushed forward and self-published the book anyway. What began as a passion project for me has grown into something so much more. Sometimes, all it takes is one decision, one action, to completely change the trajectory of your life.

I have never been afraid to be different or believed that negative is the only option. To me, it is about being true to who I am and what feels right to me. There has only ever been one negative review of any of my books. I took that one and turned it into one of my favorite series I have written yet, called Happy Thoughts.

That series was the first one to not just make me excited but also nervous. My style of writing is in first-person narration. That series has a character not just with autism, but who is nonverbal. She narrates through thought bubbles. There is always a way; is one of my favorite sayings I live by.

I decided to tackle this because I have not seen any other books like it in publication. The one thing that kept running through my head was that so many loved my books because they could see themselves in them. I'll never forget the one reading that the teacher asked me to stay back and talk to the special ed students. She said to me, *"You're like a celebrity to them. They can see themselves in your books".* That was the biggest compliment to me. The risk of backlash from any community was worth those smiling faces.

In this journey, I've made incredible author friends whom I learn from and collaborate with. I also work with the amazing and talented Brainstorm Productions. The organization employs individuals with Autism to work in animation. They have now illustrated and put together almost eighty percent of my books with no sign of slowing down.

Being open and accepting has been something that was always just easy.

Going against the grain and doing what made me happy rather than going with the crowd or trend is too. Now, being able to show that side of me has brought out the leader in me. It has brought positive changes to others' lives and my own.

Following my dream and passion has turned into a blessing I am thankful for. Publishing that first book has led to so much. I hosted an award-winning podcast for three years. That's how I met the incredibly talented Brainstorm Productions. One connection leads to another. I always tell my students, No is not forever, and a negative does not always have to stay that way. There is always a way to turn it around and make it positive. Writing has shown me that possibilities are endless, and dreams can come true.

Connect With Lisa

Facebook: booksbylisajacovsky
Instagram/Threads: diverseinkbooks
TikTok: lisajayauthor
www.diverseinkbooks.my.canva.site

SHOP NOW

Empowering Women through Wellness and Self-Care

SHE
glows

HANNA OLIVAS
Along With 26 Inspiring Authors

GRAB YOUR COPY NOW

SHE GLOWS: Empowering Women Through Wellness and Self-Care is a radiant collection of stories and strategies from women who've made wellness a priority—and transformed their lives in the process. Through real experiences, expert insights, and practical tools, this empowering book shows how self-care is not selfish, but essential. From mindfulness and movement to nutrition and boundary-setting, these stories remind us that true glow comes from within. You are not alone—and these women prove that healing, balance, and joy are all within reach when you choose to care for yourself first.

amazon.com **SHE RISES STUDIOS**

she♥wins
WOMEN'S NETWORK

Elevate your business with the power of community.

Get access to the tools, connections, and support you need to grow—with a circle of women who truly get it.

WHAT'S INCLUDED

- Strategic networking & mentorship
- Expert-led masterclasses & exclusive resources
- Member spotlights, VIP perks & more

Join for just
$87/MONTH
no contracts, cancel anytime.

www.shewinswomensnetwork.com

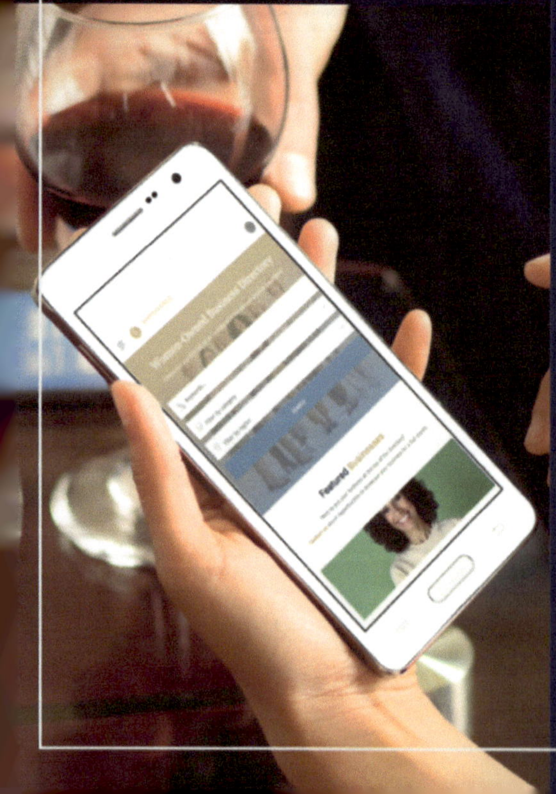

EMPOWERED
V E N T U R E S

Support women.
Discover local.
Shop with purpose.

- ☑ Discover & support women-owned businesses in every city
- ☑ Shop with purpose—locally and while you travel
- ☑ Share the power of women-owned with your network
- ☑ Join the movement—get listed, get seen, get supported
- ☑ Be the reason women-owned businesses thrive

GET LISTED
Memberships starting at $5 a month
FREE to search directory

SCAN NOW TO SIGN UP!

womenowned-business.com

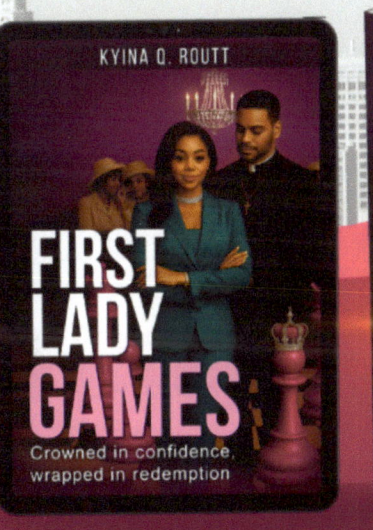

THE POWER OF WORDS:

Her Passion, Her Purpose

By Nikki Girard

Sparked by passion and a keen awareness of the transformative power of words, Nikki Girard sets the writing world ablaze.

Eager to inspire change and elevate her brand, she's excited to continuing to share her journey in upcoming features, prominent magazines, book releases, and publications.

Speaking on topics such as leadership, manifestation, mindset, personal & business growth.

Forging deep connections with readers, harnessing the magnetic force of publishing, effectively creating an unstoppable platform that reaches, educates, and inspires a wider audience.

The Power of Publishing
Publishing expands your reach, fostering collaborations and media coverage.

Build a loyal following, creating meaningful connections and a thriving platform for creative expression.

Explore formats and find the ideal platform for your content, whether it's a blog, social media, magazines, or traditional publishing houses.

Understanding your audience and tailoring content is crucial for successful publishing.

Selecting the perfect medium ensures your work successfully reaches its intended audience and maximizes impact.

From Impact to Inspiration: The Visionary Legacy of Nikki Girard
Welcome to the *'Freedom Portal,'* where the High AF Advantage empowers you to unleash your full manifestation potential.

Meet Nikki Girard a visionary, 4-time Award-Winning entrepreneur, exponential transformation & manifestation expert & Creator of the groundbreaking—High AF Advantage.

Discover Nikki's holistic method for self-mastery and success, transcending trends with unique techniques.

Shatter money codes, limitations, bending reality and enabling you to manifest your boldest dreams.

Experience a potent, transformative approach through her—High AF Advantage: 1-1 VIP Exclusive experience or upcoming Group program designed for unparalleled growth & transformation.

A few of Nikki's many accomplishments include—Force Awards awardee-Top 10 Entrepreneurs to Watch 2025 & Force Awards Nominee: Top 10 High-Impact Coach Award 2025–Force Magazine

Cast your: Vote for Nikki today!
Nikki's also the Founder & Mastermind Host of the newly launched—High AF Advantage: Life & Biz Hub, an Elite Exclusive Clubhouse Community.

Join Nikki—Experience a transformative journey with Nikki to unlock your true potential, using a powerful blend of mindset, EQ, manifestation, self-love, science, and more.

And...if you want to begin your journey towards a brighter future, and perhaps even become her next million-dollar success story connect with Nikki, apply now!

Unleash Your Voice : Ignite Your Publishing Journey
If you have a powerful message to share, now is the time to unleash your voice and ignite your publishing journey.

By taking action, you can make a meaningful impact on others while elevating your brand, significantly expanding your reach & visibility.

Remember, your words hold the potential to inspire transformation and touch lives in profound ways.

Embrace the power of publishing and watch as your influence grows, creating a lasting legacy of inspiration and positive change.

Nikki has been fortunate to explore various avenues in the publishing world, from contributing to prominent best selling magazines, Pragma Journal as well as being a 3-time #1 International & 4-time #1 Amazon best selling author.

She's excited for her solo book—High AF Advantage:Your Quantum Core Blueprint to Success, releasing summer 2025.

Also Keep an eye out...her upcoming collaborative books—Mindset Mastery, Becoming Iconic, Mind Over Matter, Unleasher Voice & The Untold Story to name a few.

Nikki's publishing journey has been filled with enriching experiences, remarkable connections & networking opportunities.

Make it Happen
So, if you're inspired to embark on your path to becoming a published author—connect with She Rises Studios.

Experience: exceptional expert guidance, support, resources, step by step process with team work & collaboration...ensuring a seamless publishing experience from start to finish.

Just say...Nikki Girard referred you and be treated like gold!!

Learn more about Nikki's transformative coaching and entrepreneurial services at: High AF Advantage Success-Impact-Legacy

Remember...you matter & your message matters!

Connect With Nikki

www.highafadvantage.com
www.clubhouse.com/house/high-af-advantage
www.facebook.com/nikki.girard.311
www.linkedin.com/in/nikki-girard-962601207
www.instagram.com/nikki.girard.311

THE HIDDEN WRITER IN US ALL

By Hannah Darby

I believe there is an author inside all of us trapped by fear..... A fear of sharing your story. A fear of the blank white page staring back at you. A fear of writer's block a brain empty of ideas. A fear that your message will be lost in translation. A fear that I'm not good enough to be in print. A fear that no-one will ever read your words. Breaking through that fear is hard, but if I can do it you can too!

The Girl Who Dreamed
You see, there was once a little girl who loved reading books. She spent hours lost in the worlds created by different writers, hours learning something new, expanding her little mind. She loved the whole experience. Snuggling down somewhere comfy, the smell of the pages as she turned them, the feeling of the paper in her hands. She would always have a book with her. It was her favourite way to fill in time. She said to herself, *'I would love to write a book one day... but I don't think it will ever happen'.*

See, she dreamed of becoming an author one day. Dreamed of seeing her words in print. She felt it would always be a dream. However, I'm pleased to say she was very wrong.

That little girl would be so proud of the woman she has become today. That little girl was me.

The Woman Who Wins
I still can't quite believe the journey I have been on. From a life-long dream to the reality of becoming an international bestselling author, not just once but multiple times. I have proudly co-authored 4 books out now on Amazon - She Defies: Powerful Stories of Overcoming, She Wins: Nice Girls Finish First, Her Path to Entrepreneurship: A Journey of Courage Vision, and Success and When Hearts Heal. I have another book out later this month - Unleash Her: The next Chapter Begins.

I am signed for more co-authored projects out later this year and into next year. Even more exciting is that I have signed up to do my own book so watch this space...

I absolutely love reading and writing. The expression of ones-self through words is truly magical. There is so much healing to be found in giving your thoughts form on paper.

Stories For The Heart, From The Heart
All my chapters are raw, real, and straight from the heart. They are an expression of my soul. A testament to my journey. A dialogue of my struggles. I want to give you the tools I have learned along the way in blood, sweat and tears, so that you don't ever feel as low as I did. Remember you are never alone. I aim to inspire you that no matter how hard it gets, no matter what you have been through, if you stay true to your values, believe in yourself and never give up on your dreams, you can make your dreams your reality too.

If I Can Do It, You can Too
We all start with a blank page. But your story does matter. Your words and dreams matter. I would love for you to pick up a pen and give it a go. Even if no-one else ever reads it. Give yourself the opportunity for growth. You see it's all about mindset.... Turn your fear and nerves into excitement. Excitement for the opportunity ahead. Excitement for inspiring others through your words. Just let your words flow. Remember we all start with an empty page.

Connect With Hannah

www.healingwithhannah.co.uk
www.accph.org.uk/united-kingdom/martley/therapists-and-coaches/hannah-darby
www.facebook.com/hannahsdarby
www.instagram.com/healingwithhannahd
www.linkedin.com/in/hannahdarbyhealingwithhannah

INSPIRE
EMPOWER
EDUCATE

GRAB YOUR COPY NOW

She Knows Her Worth: Empowerment through Self-Respect and Confidence is a heartfelt collection of stories from women who've faced self-doubt—and found their way to unshakable confidence. Through honest reflections and practical wisdom, these women share how they built boundaries, silenced inner critics, and learned to celebrate their worth. This empowering book is both a guide and a companion for anyone ready to embrace their true value and live boldly. You are not alone—and these stories are proof that confidence grows when you choose to honor your worth, every single day.

amazon.com   **SHE RISES** STUDIOS

RISING FROM THE FLOOR:

A Widow's Journey Through Grief, Healing, and Hope

By Layla Beth Munk

In February of 2018, life as I knew it came to a screeching halt. My husband, Bret, who'd struggled with depression and mental health issues, ended his own life. I had no idea what I was supposed to do or even how to just continue on. All these years later, I look back at that version of me in a heap on the floor, unable or even just unwilling to move from the spot, and I picture myself telling me that it's going to be okay. It's going to get better. Some of the best moments of your life are yet to come.

My journey has not been without struggle, but honestly, whose hasn't? Life is rarely ever what we see on social media, with perfect-looking people in perfect-looking places living perfect lives. That's precisely the reason why I chose to showcase my healing journey in all its splendid chaos. I decided to share it all: The ugly truths. The hilarious missteps. The losses. The wins.

Since that fateful day, I have written and published three books. (And a poetry chapbook as well.) I have also been blessed with the opportunity to blog twice monthly for Hope For Widows Foundation, where I share what I've learned as a widow with others seeking comfort. Most importantly, I've watched our daughter blossom into a lovely young woman, despite her own trauma and devastation. Both of my children have been the biggest blessing to me in all of this, which is another thing I tell the version of myself still on the floor after Bret's death—they need you, and you need them. Together, you will rise above all of this.

It took being stripped of what I perceived to be my security to remember just who I am. I won't lie—there are regrets about wasted years and things that were precious to me from which I had willingly walked away, to put Bret's happiness above my own. At half a century old now, sometimes I wonder if I can get those parts of me back. Whether I can or can't remains to be seen, but I am sure trying.

Focusing on my writing has really helped bring it all into focus. Memories have been unlocked. Random musings have made me smile. Recollections have been turned into stories; tales that will hopefully bring smiles to the faces of those who read them. Laughter, as well. Because who am I without my sense of humor? Sometimes that humor may tend toward dark, but I've come to know that this can be quite normal for widows. There is some trace of humor in nearly everything I write. Even the sad stuff. Because laughter truly is the best medicine.

I know, without a doubt, that I was put here, in this life, to share my words and to comfort as many people as I can. There are many more stories in me that I am going to allow to emerge. Whether they may be humorous online shorts, full books, or bi-monthly blogs for the bereaved, I will write them. It is an honor and a privilege when people take the time out of their busy lives to read my work.

My books are available on Amazon, but can also be found through my website, laylabeth.net, along with other information and various links. The award-winning Hope For Widows blog can be found at hopeforwidows.org/blog, and there are multiple contributors, not just me. Through grief, some beautiful things can be born. I am so grateful that I was able to learn this valuable lesson.

Connect With Layla

www.laylabeth.net
www.hopeforwidows.org/author/laylabethmunk
www.facebook.com/laylabeth
www.instagram.com/ladylaylabeth
Threads: @ladylabeth

By Katy Anne Brack

GENTLE PARENTING OR GRACE-FILLED PARENTING

Recent parenting experts tout a new framework called "Gentle Parenting." Gentle Parenting emphasizes a nurturing approach to raising children, focusing on connection, empathy, and mutual respect. It prioritizes understanding a child's emotions and needs, and it uses guidance—not punishment. This model aims to infuse more love, compassion, and patience into the parent-child relationship than past parenting models, and it places ownership on the child to regulate their emotions and reactions to life. When we are hyper-focused on empathy and the validation of feelings, we create a few issues.

One, we give our children a false sense of entitlement by allowing them to believe all of their feelings are valid. Yes, their feelings are real—but no, not all feelings are true or good. The size and accuracy of our feelings ought to be appropriate to the situation at hand, and filtered—as Christians—through the lens of Scripture.

Two, this model of parenting gives our children full autonomy before they are ready and blurs the line between parent and child. Our relationship with them ought to reflect our relationship with our Heavenly Father: loving, but marked by clear boundary lines that have real consequences and blessings.

As an alternative to Gentle Parenting, we ought to employ Grace-Filled Parenting. Grace-Filled Parenting still brings to the table compassion for our children, intentional listening, and the instilling of ownership over their actions. But it also clarifies the distinction between parent and child, and emphasizes the necessary vertical dimension of parenting.

It establishes wise boundaries that allow children to feel more at ease in exploring their space, offering them not only natural consequences and rewards that prepare them for adulthood, but also parent-given ones that seek to conform them into the image of Christ.

Grace-Filled Parenting teaches that all of our very real feelings ought to be evaluated through Scripture and prayer. We are not to be controlled by our feelings. Our feelings—like us—are fallible, and are to be tamed by the Spirit.

Through Scripture and our personal vulnerability as mothers, Grace-Filled Parenting models openness to imperfection and a rhythm of forgiveness. We can be honest about our errors, seek forgiveness when we wrong our children, and model reconciliation well. Our children need to know how to heal relationships and problem-solve in a safe, God-honoring way.

In the same vein, we want to give our children freedom as is appropriate. We want them to become the decision-makers when they are ready and can be trusted to do so wisely. "One who is faithful in a very little is also faithful in much" (Luke 16:10).

Grace-Filled Parenting is hard. Our goal as mothers is to serve our children well, root them in Christ, and always look to the Lord. For us, this requires intentionality, vulnerability, and constant sanctification. Not an easy road—but God has gone before us in every step and has given us amazing brains and bodies that can put His tools to use. His Word, His Church, and the Holy Spirit are our network of support!

We will never fully "arrive" as mothers on this side of Heaven, but the Lord will be with us—and with our children—as we learn and grow throughout motherhood, a motherhood marked by Grace-Filled Parenting.

"Do not provoke your children to anger, but bring them up in the discipline and instruction of the Lord." Ephesians 6:4

Katy Anne Brack is a mother of four, a wife of nineteen years, and the author of Mom Guilt: Moving From Guilt to the Gospel. She lives in Cypress, TX, and would be honored to connect with you.

Connect With Katy

www.linkedin.com/in/katybrack1983
www.facebook.com/katy.a.brack

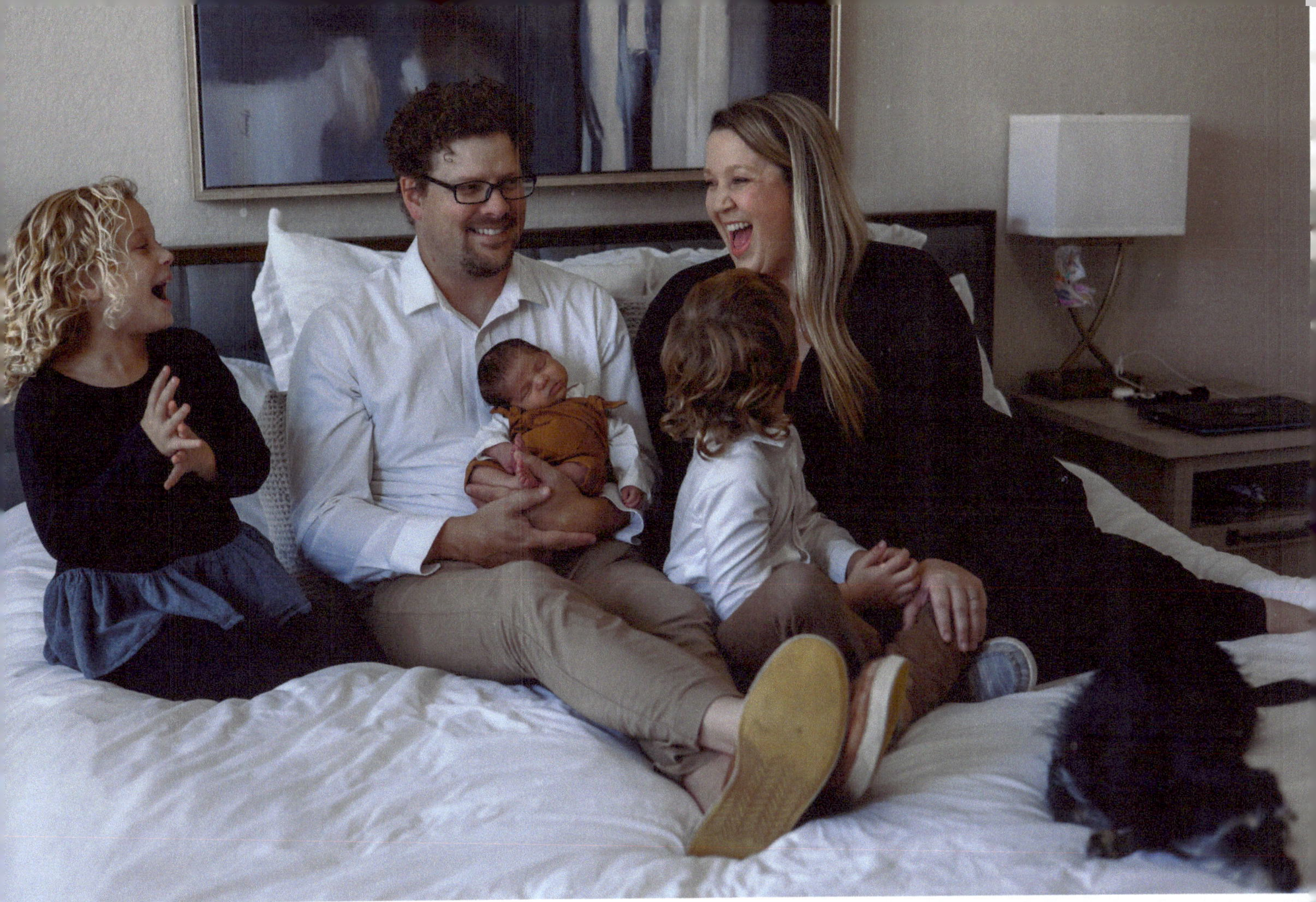

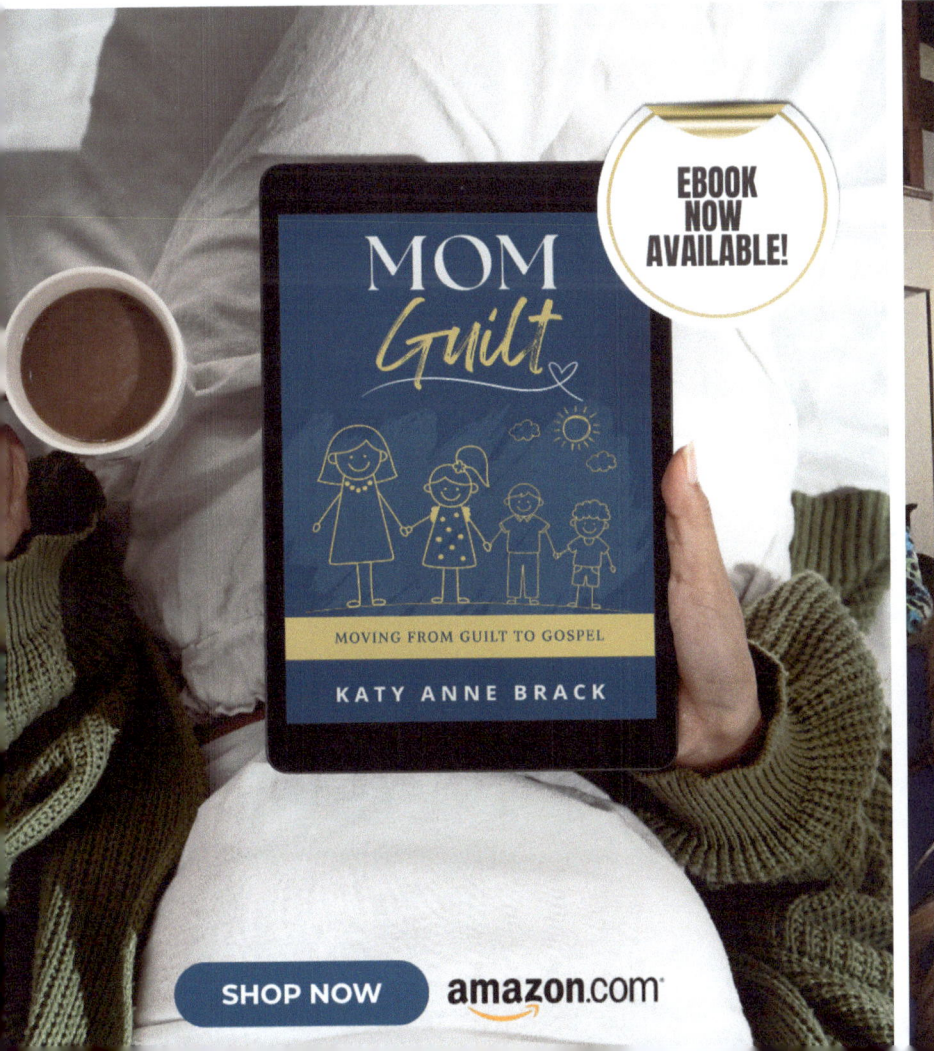

EBOOK
NOW
AVAILABLE!
MOM
Guilt
MOVING FROM GUILT TO GOSPEL
KATY ANNE BRACK
SHOP NOW
amazon.com

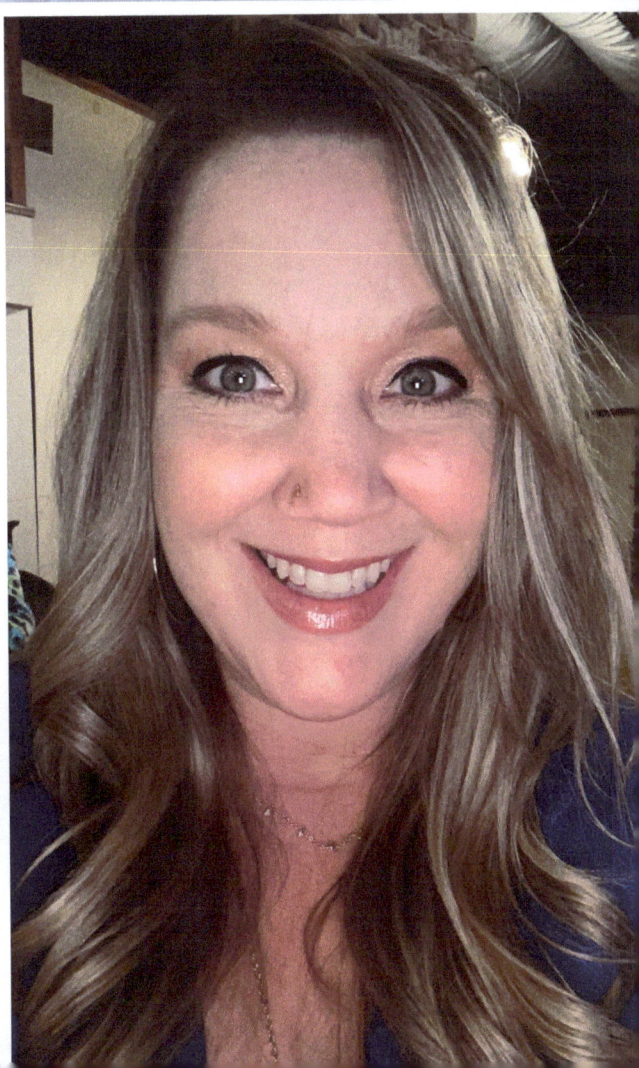

JOIN THE SRS COMMUNITY

WHERE WOMEN RISE TOGETHER!

Connect. Empower. Thrive. Whether you're an entrepreneur, professional, or simply seeking inspiration, **this is your space to grow!**

- Daily Motivation
- Expert Insights
- Sisterhood & Support

You don't have to do it alone—let's rise together!

JOIN NOW!

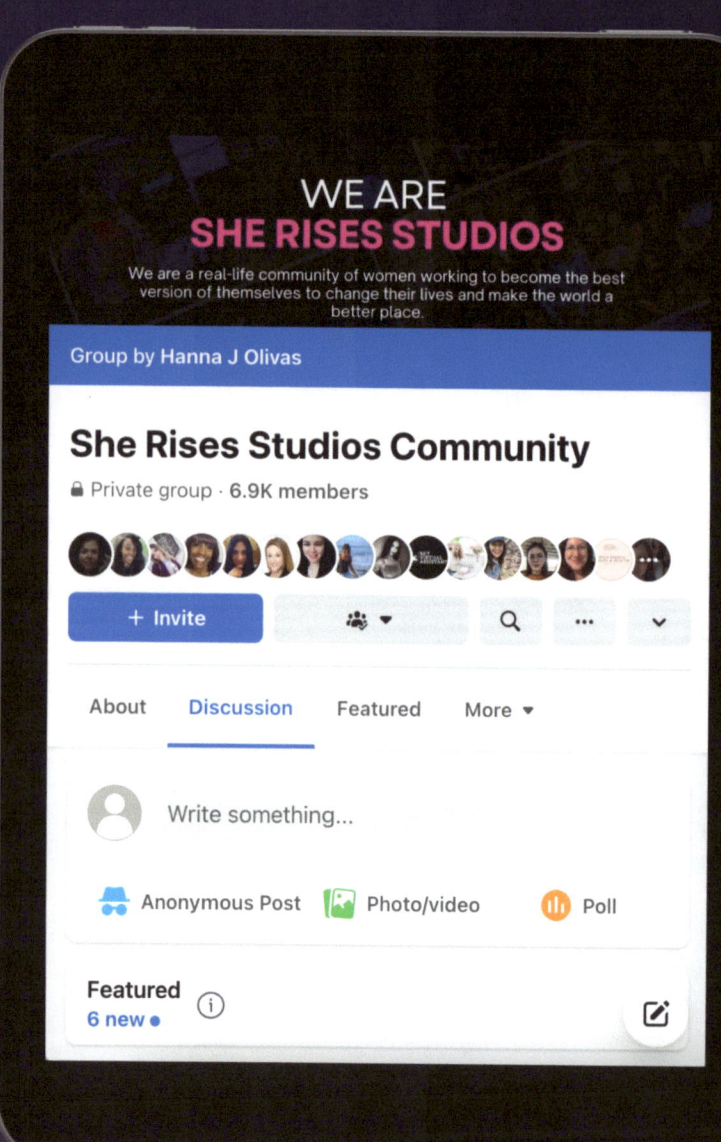

TRANSFORMING
PAIN INTO
PURPOSE

By Tanisha Mackin

Like many children, I envisioned a future of fame or a career in healthcare. Yet, the winding road of life rarely aligns with our early ambitions. Though I secretly yearned to be an entrepreneur, self-doubt about my skills held me back. It was in the wake of my husband's tragic death on our one-year wedding anniversary that I finally found my life's purpose.

In the wake of my husband's unexpected death and while battling colon cancer, I found solace and purpose in writing. Though it had always been a passion since high school, a friend's suggestion to document the preceding years of my life truly sparked my journey. My first book's success encouraged me to keep writing, leading to speaking engagements where I discovered my love for the entire process of writing and publishing. As I continued to write and support other widows, I began receiving requests for publishing assistance. This demand ultimately led to the creation of Tanisha Mackin Publishing, where I now offer a variety of packages to help clients bring their own books to life and share their stories through writing.

Many aspiring authors had powerful stories but lacked the time or writing skills to tell them. Recognizing this need, I expanded my publishing offerings to include ghostwriting services. Sharing these testimonies and stories became my purpose, helping me navigate my own pain. Today, my full-service publishing company has proudly released over 100 books across all genres, transforming clients into bestselling authors. I've been dedicated to the publishing business for 10 years, and I absolutely love it.

Today, my company, Exclusive Publishing by Tanisha Mackin (formerly Tanisha Mackin Publishing), stands as a luxury publishing house dedicated to meeting my clients' unique needs. Our comprehensive packages include ghostwriting services, branding, promotion, media features, and VIP treatment.

I've also expanded my business to include Exclusive Virtual Assistant by Tanisha Mackin. Through this service, I provide clients with essential administrative and creative support, covering everything from social media content and promotional flyers to newsletters and more.

My passion for travel has also led me to become a travel writer, sharing my experiences with the world—especially alongside my two children, whom I adore traveling with.

It hasn't been an easy road, but I've transformed my pain into purpose. With strength and perseverance, I've built a successful publishing company, and I'm just getting started.

Connect With Tanisha

www.linktr.ee/tanishamackin
www.instagram.com/ExclusiveVirtualAssistantbyTM
www.instagram.com/ExclusivePublishingbyTM

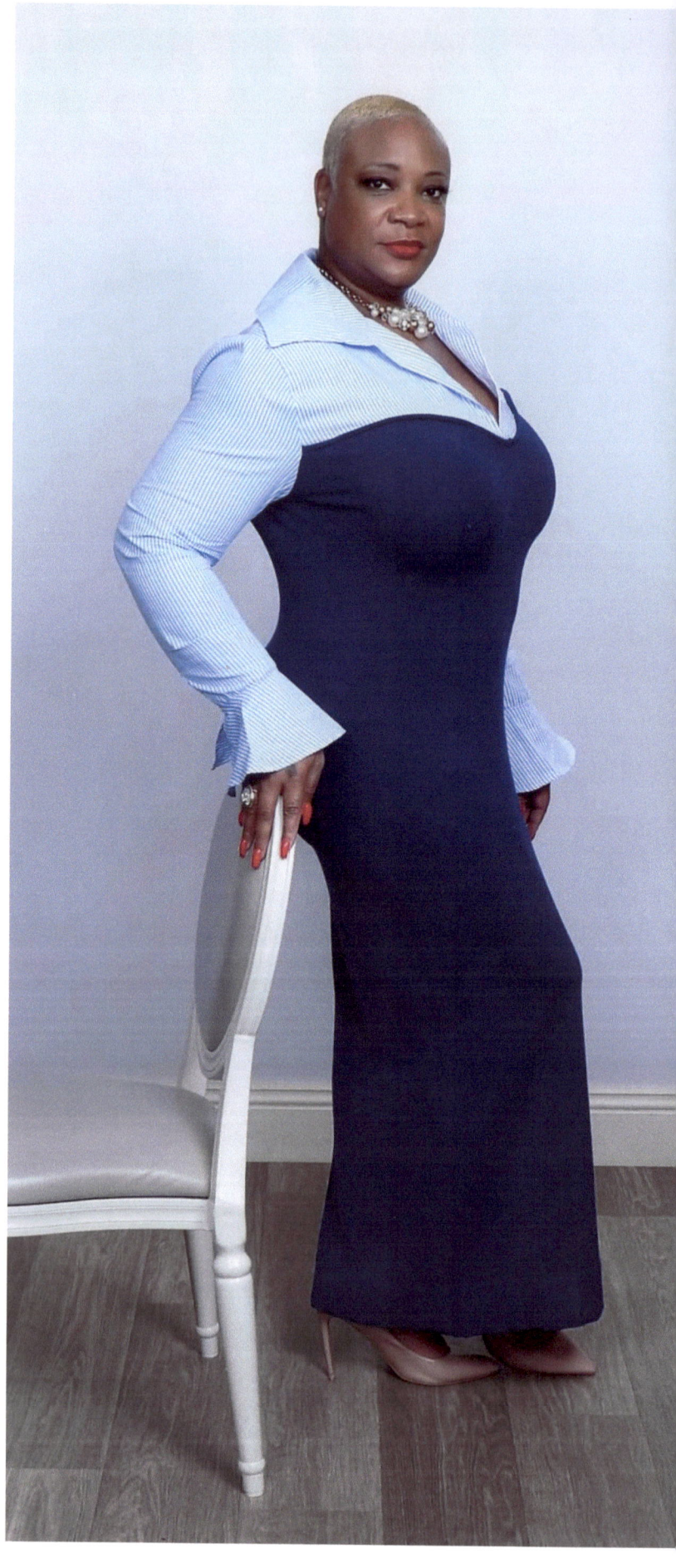

INKUBATOR

GRAB YOUR COPY NOW

Her Path to Entrepreneurship: A Journey of Courage, Vision, and Success shares the real, unfiltered stories of women who turned ambition into action—and built thriving businesses on their own terms. From startup struggles to leadership wins, these powerful journeys offer insight, strategy, and the motivation to keep going. Whether you're just beginning or growing your next big idea, this collection proves that success comes in many forms—and every path is worth celebrating. You are not alone—and these stories show that with courage and vision, anything is possible.

amazon.com   SHE RISES STUDIOS

FROM MY CIRCLE TO THE PAGE:

Writing What Community Gave Me

By Tomeko Brown

Growing up, I learned the importance of community. Whether it's the love of family, friends, teachers, or even strangers, a strong community helps shape us. It provides the support we need to grow, and it's especially important for children to recognize those around them who help them to thrive and reach their full potential.

I was about eight years old when, just a few days after Christmas, my family's home burned down. My brother, who was about four at the time, and I stood on our neighbor's porch, watching as firefighters worked hard to control the flames. Unfortunately, we lost everything. All we had was the clothes we were wearing. That night, my family and I moved in with our great uncle to prepare ourselves for the long haul of rebuilding.

But that's when I witnessed the true strength of the community. In a matter of 48 hours, it seemed like the support of family, friends, and total strangers came to the rescue. Bags of clothes, toys, household necessities, money—you name it—poured in, providing the strength and compassion we needed at that moment.

Yes, the material support made a huge difference, but it was the emotional support that mattered most. People came together to make sure we had what we needed and, more importantly, to remind us that we were not alone.

Looking back, I see how the kindness of others carried us through one of the hardest times in our lives. It's a reminder that when everything else feels uncertain, the strength of the community can be the thing that keeps us going.

This experience, as well as others, is what brought me to this moment—a voice to keep uplifting the importance of community, especially to children, through storytelling. As a mom and a former educator, it's important that children continue to understand the strength of the community-- the people who help them reach their goals, support them through challenges, and help them see their full potential.

One of my favorite books, both as a child and still today, is Charlotte's Web by E.B. White. It beautifully illustrates the values of compassion, friendship, and community. These same themes are at the heart of my recent book, An Instrument for Florenda. In it, we see the strong friendship between Lilly and Nate, who stand by Florenda and encourage her. We see the kindness of neighbors like Mr. and Mrs. Lyles and the unconditional love from her adopted mother.

Together, these individuals help Florenda grow and achieve her dream of learning to play the clarinet. They were her community.

Both books show us that we don't reach our goals alone. Whether it's a friend, a neighbor—or in Wilbur's case, a spider—sometimes we all need a little help to become the best version of ourselves. And like the characters in these stories, we all have a community of, seen and unseen, who help us along the way.

That's why I want young readers to connect with Florenda's story in a real way. I hope they can see parts of themselves in the characters and recognize the community of people around them who are cheering them on and supporting their growth. Florenda's journey is one many kids can relate to, and I hope it encourages them to keep going, even when things get tough.

Connect With Tomeko

www.tomekobrown.com/about-me
www.instagram.com/tomeko_brown_author
www.x.com/ttbrown122
www.linkedin.com/in/tomekobrown

PINK, PURPOSEFUL AND PROFITABLE:

Living Your Flamingo Advantage in a World of Crocs and Sharks

By Katie Hornor

When I started my first business from a dusty corner of Mexico with a baby on my hip and a vision in my heart, I didn't look like what the world told me a *"successful entrepreneur"* should be. I didn't have a business degree, a corporate background, or a sleek brand. What I had was something far more powerful: purpose.

Today, I'm an international keynote speaker, founder of The Flamingo Advantage®, and recently honored as the 2025 Visionary Coach of the Year by Insider Weekly. My books have earned multiple Book Awards. And I'm still that same woman—boldly living out my God-given purpose in full flamingo color.

Here's the truth: the world is full of crocs—copycats who blend in—and sharks—those who lead by fear, competition, or aggression. But flamingos? Flamingos stand tall. They gather in supportive communities. They are unashamed of their color. And most importantly, they live aligned with their design.

If you want to lead a business that's both purposeful and profitable, it's time to embrace your Flamingo Advantage. Here's how.

1. Show Up in Full Color

Flamingos don't ask permission to be pink. They don't apologize for standing out. How often do you dim your light to fit in with the industry norm?

Bold leadership starts with owning your uniqueness. That includes your personality, your faith, your voice, and your values. Your quirks aren't liabilities—they're your edge. When I began including flamingo metaphors into my trainings, some said it was too *"out there."* But those same metaphors are now what I'm known for. They've opened the door to stages, podcast interviews, and even a billboard in Time Square.

2. Protect Your Purpose

Flamingos often stand on one leg—not because they're quirky, but to conserve energy and allow them to stay aligned with their design. You too must protect your energy and your purpose.

That means setting boundaries around your time and attention. It means saying no to opportunities that look good but don't feel aligned. And it means anchoring your business decisions in your core mission, not the marketplace noise.

In my coaching work with successful business owners and event hosts, I see this repeatedly: the more alignement with their divine purpose and mission, the more profit follows—because their message carries conviction, not confusion.

3. Gather with the Right Flock

Flamingos thrive in flocks. And yet, too many entrepreneurs try to do business alone, or worse, they surround themselves with *"crocs"* who don't celebrate their differences.

If you're called to do business differently, you need a community that honors that. That's why I created the BOLD program—a safe space where leaders can grow without compromising their faith, family or values. Find your people. It changes everything.

4. Bold Is Better Than Big

Success isn't about being the loudest in the room—it's about being the clearest in your conviction.

When I began speaking about blending faith and business—in boardrooms, stages, podcasts, even TEDx—I wasn't the biggest name. But I was bold. That boldness has led to more visibility, trust and clients than any marketing tactic I've ever tried.

Bold doesn't mean brash or obnoxious. It means being brave enough to live intentionally and with integrity.

In a world full of crocs and sharks, your greatest advantage is being a flamingo: uniquely created, fully expressed, and faithfully aligned with your calling.

Be pink. Be purposeful. Be profitable.
And above all, be bold enough to stand in the place only you were created to fill.

Connect With Katie

www.theflamingoadvantage.com
www.youtube.com/@katiehornorflamingoadvantage
www.instagram.com/katiehornor
www.linkedin.com/in/katiehornor

she wins
WOMEN'S NETWORK

SPEAK AT SHE WINS GLOBAL SUMMIT 2025

NOVEMBER 6–7, 2025 | LAS VEGAS, NV

The She Wins Global Summit 2025 is calling all bold, passionate, and purpose-driven women to take the stage. This powerful **2-day event** will bring together over **500 women leaders, entrepreneurs, and professionals** from around the world for a transformational experience. As a speaker, you'll share your knowledge, story, or expertise in front of a **global audience**—while gaining massive visibility, media exposure, and high-level networking opportunities.

Topics include finance, leadership, business growth, mental health, branding, AI, wellness, innovation, diversity, public speaking, and more. Speaker benefits include a premier speaking slot, TV broadcast of your talk on FENIX TV, media features, red carpet experience, a premium swag bag, gourmet lunch for both days, custom promo graphics, and two full event passes—**valued at over $2,000**, all included with your speaker package.

If you're ready to lead, inspire, and make a real impact, this is your moment. Share your voice, elevate your brand, and join a global movement of unstoppable women.

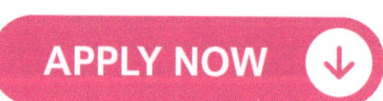
APPLY NOW

 https://form.jotform.com/250646617740156

I WAS BEATEN, BROKEN, AND SHATTERED. BUT I ROSE LOUD ENOUGH FOR THE ONES STILL WHISPERING.

By Victoria Cuore

Victoria Cuore shouldn't be alive.

She was beaten while pregnant. Shattered by violence so extreme that it left her with over 100 surgeries and the loss of her arm below the elbow. Her abuser tried to break everything: her bones, her spirit, her future. But the one thing he couldn't silence was her voice.

And today, that voice is a lifeline for millions.

Victoria's daughter, Faith, was born prematurely due to the trauma she suffered in the womb. By her mother's side, Faith has already endured more than 50 surgeries of her own. But this mother-daughter duo didn't just survive, they've turned their pain into a purpose that's touching lives across the globe.

With her husband Michael, a proud U.S. military veteran who shares her heart for service, Victoria founded A Contagious Smile, born from the ashes of personal tragedy. Together, the three of them, Victoria, Michael, and Faith, have created a movement of healing that now includes a brand-new initiative: The A Contagious Smile Online Academy.

This isn't your typical education platform. It's a sanctuary for the wounded. A lifeline for those who feel forgotten. Designed specifically for survivors, special needs families, veterans, and individuals in recovery, the academy offers free and low-cost trauma-informed courses rooted in lived experience, not theory.

Because Victoria knows what it feels like to have no one. She's lived through the kind of hurt that money can't fix and systems often ignore. And she's made a vow:
No one who's ready to heal will ever be turned away.

If someone shows up ready to begin again, A Contagious Smile will open the door. But the help doesn't stop there.

Victoria is the author of dozens of healing-focused books, journals, and trauma workbooks, including her gut-wrenching memoir Who Kicked First and its powerful prequel Narc Narc Who's There. Through her writing, she gives survivors the words they didn't know how to say, and the strength to say them out loud.

She's also the voice behind the globally ranked podcast, A Contagious Smile, now in the top 1% worldwide. Each episode is raw, real, and brave, featuring stories of abuse, resilience, parenting, trauma, disability, and survival. It's not about perfection. It's about connections. And for many listeners, it's the first time they've truly felt seen.

Victoria and her family receive no monetary compensation for their work. Their payment? The messages from people who say, *I didn't give up because of you.* The smile of someone who no longer feels invisible. The moment a whisper turns into a roar.
The A Contagious Smile Online Academy was built for those still whispering. For those who've survived the worst and are ready to step into their healing journey.

If you've ever felt broken, this is proof that healing is still possible.

If you've ever wanted to help someone find their voice again, this is your chance.

Help others by sponsoring a scholarship. Sign up for a course. All of their courses are low-cost, with dozens being FREE, and new courses are added weekly.

Simply remember, even the most shattered lives can rise and rise loud enough for the ones still whispering.

Join today *https://acontagioussmile.mn.co/*

A Contagious Smile Unstoppable Podcast

EVERY SMILE TELLS A STORY

Unstoppable

A CONTAGIOUS SMILE'S MICHAEL AND VICTORIA DISCUSS HOT TOPICS IN A MANNER MOST WON'T

Connect With Victoria

www.acontagioussmile.mn.co
www.acontagioussmile.com
www.podcasts.apple.com/us/podcast/a-contagious-smile-podcast/id1617838625
www.facebook.com/profile.php?id=61576680343801
www.buymeacoffee.com/victoriacuore

Mastering Risk, Growth, and Value Creation in Entrepreneurship

HER
Bold
BUSINESS MOVES

HANNA OLIVAS

ALONG WITH 16 INSPIRING AUTHORS

GRAB YOUR COPY NOW

Her Bold Business Moves: Mastering Risk, Growth, and Value Creation in Entrepreneurship is an empowering collection of stories and strategies from women who've taken bold leaps—and built thriving businesses on their terms. From embracing risk to scaling with purpose, these trailblazing entrepreneurs share how they turned challenges into opportunities and vision into impact. With practical insights and real-world lessons, this book is your roadmap to making confident moves in business and life. You are not alone—and these stories prove that boldness, backed by purpose, is the key to lasting success.

amazon.com   SHE RISES STUDIOS

Join Our Retreat

RENEWED HORIZONS RETREAT TURKEY OCTOBER 18TH-25TH 2025
ALL THINGS ARE POSSIBLE—EVEN AFTER LOSS.

GRIEF COMES IN MANY FORMS—DEATH, DIVORCE, ILLNESS, IDENTITY SHIFTS.
THIS RETREAT IS A SACRED SPACE TO SOFTEN THE ACHE AND REDISCOVER YOUR LIGHT.

JOIN US FOR A HEART-LED JOURNEY OF HEALING, REMEMBRANCE, AND RENEWAL.

GUIDED MEDITATIONS & SOUL JOURNALING
REIKI, TAROT, AND INTUITIVE ENERGY HEALING
BREATHWORK, NATURE CONNECTION

YOU ARE NOT BROKEN. YOU ARE BECOMING.
LET THIS BE YOUR RETURN TO PEACE.

NIKKI HOLDS SPACE WITH HEART AND SOUL. AS A SEASONED RETREAT HOST
THERAPEUTIC COACH, AUTHOR, AND SPEAKER,
SHE BRINGS DEEP COMPASSION AND LIVED WISDOM TO EVERY STEP OF YOUR JOURNEY.

ALONGSIDE NIKKI, YOU'LL BE SUPPORTED BY REIKI MASTER ANGIE AND SPIRITUAL MENTOR LISA
TWO GIFTED HEALERS DEDICATED TO HOLDING SACRED SPACE FOR YOUR TRANSFORMATION.

LIMITED SPACES—RESERVE YOUR PLACE AT NIKKIHILLHOUSE.COM

TAKE THE ROAD LESS TRAVELED WITH CHILDREN'S BOOK AUTHOR

By Shannon Mori

Self-published authors enjoy taking the road less traveled, and the internationally sold, successful self-published author, Shannon Mori, continuously takes that road. This road less traveled has increasingly become a way for aspiring authors and entrepreneurs to seek new revenue streams and decisive advantages. *"The number of self-published books has increased 264% in the last five years,"* according to Wordsrated. With this increase of self-published books, independent authors are proving to thrive, as well as earn significantly more than their traditionally published counterparts. While self-publishing gives the freedom for writers to take the reins of their literary career, it also demands a strategic method to become successful. Mori has taken those reins of her own literary career with her children's book series, Pawsome Pals.

One of the crucial steps to success as an independent author is to know your purpose. Mori's Pawsome Pals book series was created to help children navigate big feelings. Using a warm narrative that fosters empathy, her books deliver comfort and support. The series invites children to talk about their feelings and creates lifelong benefits of building better relationships, higher self-esteem, and a stronger foundation for learning. The inspiration for her books is to offer encouragement to all children, and after reading a Pawsome Pals book, children and their parents will feel better about themselves and the world around them. Her inspiration behind all she does is her own two incredibly bright children.

With a commitment to foster connection and understanding, Mori's newest book, *'Puppy Day Jitters,'* released worldwide in May 2025 to popular retailers, such as Amazon, Barnes & Noble, Books-A-Million, and Walmart, contributes to the growing movement in children's books covering emotional wellbeing. With a mission to encourage discussion about the universal experience of being anxious or nervous, *'Puppy Day Jitters'* promotes empathy and addresses emotions that go along with starting something new. With back-to-school season quickly approaching, it is a perfect addition to books addressing the first day of school with the purpose of calming those first day nerves.

The message of the first book of the Pawsome Pals series, 'The Ear Bend, is to celebrate being different. It encourages discussions about embracing who you are and celebrating that we are all unique and special in our own way. According to the National Center for Youth Services, *"picture books about big feelings can be a valuable tool for helping little kids learn about their different emotions, how to identify them, and how to express them in a healthy way. As they get older, this will help them grow in self-esteem, emotional regulation, and a positive approach to managing their own feelings."* Mori's Pawsome Pals series is a perfect example of this valuable tool for children and their parents and teachers.

Mori has started work on a brand-new project, and she is looking forward to sharing more about that and what is next for the Pawsome Pals. Follow her journey and her blog, That's A'Mori, and learn more at www.shannonmori.com and on social media. She happily answers questions and mentors any future writers that are looking to start their own self-publishing career. She loves visiting classrooms, whether in person or virtually, to share her love of reading, writing, and encouraging the youngest of writers to follow their own dreams. If Mori's literary journey inspires other aspiring authors to take the reins of their own writing career and if her books offer support and comfort to young children around the world, then that is a publishing success story worth celebrating.

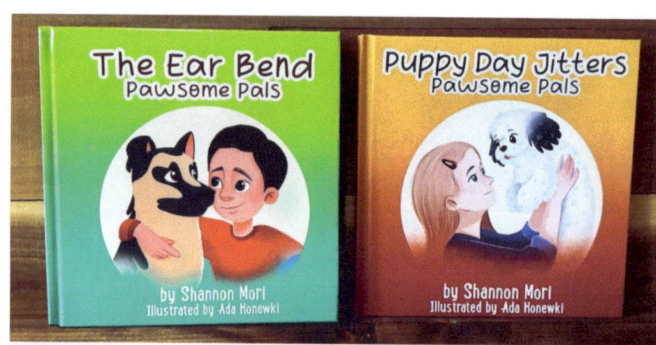

Connect With Shannon

www.shannonmori.com
www.amazon.com/stores/author/B0C1KHMW93
www.facebook.com/people/Shannon-Mori
www.instagram.com/shannonmoriauthor
www.goodreads.com/author/show/30418057.Shannon_Mori

HOLLY
COTTON

Turning Setbacks Into Strategy and Purpose Into Power

When most people think of strength, they think of muscles and motivation. But for Holly Cotton, strength is about so much more. It's about resilience, reinvention, and the unshakable will to rise even when life gives you every reason to fall.

A registered nurse, bestselling author, speaker, and cancer survivor, Holly Cotton's journey is one of transformation and intention.

Her story begins not in the spotlight, but in a moment of unimaginable vulnerability: a breast cancer diagnosis that changed everything. The physical toll was only part of the battle. What followed was an emotional and mental reset that forced Holly to rebuild from the inside out.

That life altering experience led to her first book, Strong. More Than Muscles. What began as a personal healing journey became a powerful message to the world: that true strength isn't always visible. Sometimes it's in the quiet resilience, the self-talk, the comeback. That message opened the door to a broader mission, one focused on helping others heal, grow, and reclaim their power.

Since then, Holly has authored a series of self-love and self-help books designed to empower readers through every chapter of life. Whether it's navigating heartbreak, reclaiming your worth, or learning to let go of toxic narratives, her books are bold, honest, and packed with real tools for transformation. Through them, she has become a trusted self-love facilitator, guiding others to rewrite their stories with confidence and clarity.

But her commitment to healing doesn't stop with adults. Holly also recognized the need for early intervention and support among youth facing rising mental health challenges. That's why she created Your Mind, Your Magic, a free interactive digital platform that provides children and adolescents with mental health tools, emotional support, and empowerment resources.

The site offers affirmations, journaling prompts, stress quizzes, and self-reflection activities that meet kids where they are, helping them explore their feelings, build confidence, and discover their inner magic.

With schools and families often overwhelmed, Your Mind, Your Magic fills a critical gap, offering accessible and safe support that is as engaging as it is impactful. Holly's ability to bridge adult self-empowerment with youth mental wellness makes her voice and her work uniquely powerful.

What sets Holly apart is her ability to blend inspiration with real-world strategy. Every project, from her books to her digital platforms, is grounded in the belief that your past does not define you. Your decisions do. She teaches that the experiences that tried to break you can actually become the foundation of your purpose.

Her mission is clear: to help others rise. Whether she's empowering women to love themselves fully or equipping kids with mental health tools that last a lifetime, Holly Cotton leads with heart, experience, and a fierce sense of purpose.

Holly is more than a survivor. She is a builder, a self-love advocate, and a youth mental health trailblazer. Her life is a blueprint for how to turn adversity into action and purpose into a platform that changes lives.

For anyone ready to turn passion into purpose, Holly Cotton isn't just a guide. She is the proof that it's possible.

Connect With Holly

www.hollycotton.com
www.yourmindyourmagic.com
www.instagram.com/hollycotton_
www.linkedin.com/in/holly-cotton-3342a6227
www.facebook.com/share/1LfEL9syJq

My journey as a children's Book author has been influenced greatly by my career in the field of psychology and later academia. I began my career in applied behavior analysis (ABA), where I was trained to understand and support behavior through evidence-based strategies. Working directly with children and families taught me how impactful early intervention and positive communication can be. That experience sparked a passion for helping children feel understood, which is something I later channeled into storytelling.

After being in the field for four years, I decided to pursue a PhD in ABA, where I gained extensive training in research and scientific methods. I deepened my ability to analyze human behavior, interpret data, and apply evidence-based practices. Although I ultimately chose to leave the program, the experience provided me with a strong foundation in critical thinking and communication. Sometimes you learn you need to pivot and use the skills you have learned for a different path in your career.

The skills I built continue to shape my work as a children's book author and a professor. In addition, as an author, I strive to reflect developmental and psychological principles in ways that are accessible and affirming for readers of all ages.

Those skills directly inform how I craft children's stories that are educational, inclusive, and emotionally intelligent. In addition, they would continue to influence my career as an entrepreneur and professor.

Stepping into entrepreneurship as an author was a natural extension of my academic work. It allowed me to merge research-based knowledge with creative expression. Marketing has been my only learning curve. However, with a background in research and the ability to network with more seasoned authors, I learned the skills needed to be successful as an entrepreneur. I began to reach a broader audience and advocate for topics close to my heart, like autism acceptance, emotional regulation, and kindness. Building a brand, connecting with families, and collaborating with illustrators (many of whom are individuals with autism themselves) has been a powerful way to turn my academic training into public impact.

I began my journey as a children's book author before becoming a professor. That role sharpened my ability to communicate complex concepts clearly and meaningfully as a professor. These were skills that I continue to use daily when I provide my lessons to students.

FROM ACADEMIA TO ENTREPRENEURSHIP:

My Path from ABA to successful Author and Educator

By Lisa Jacovsky M.S.

It also enhanced my ability to relate to my students and create a compassionate and comfortable setting for them.

Juggling entrepreneurship with the responsibilities of being a professor has not been easy, but it has been meaningful and worth it. It has taught me what success truly looks like, and for me, that is staying true to my purpose while adapting and growing. In both the classroom and the creative space, I've discovered that my academic foundation is not just a starting point, but a continual guide. Whether I'm teaching future professionals or writing for young readers, I've learned how to turn knowledge into impact. My goal remains the same: to use what I've learned to foster connection, empowerment, and meaningful change. Integration of skills from one career path to another looks different for everyone. However, with the motivation and confidence, anyone can do it.

Lisa
Jacovsky, PsyD

Connect With Lisa

www.diverseinkbooks.my.canva.site
Facebook: booksbylisajacovsky
Instagram: diverseinkbooks
TikTok: lisajayauthor

Personalized & Flexible Education For Grades K-8

IAOMAI ACADEMY

Unlocking Potential and Inspiring Confidence

Big Potential, Small Setting - Where Bright Minds Thrive

ABOUT US

Iaomai Academy is a K–8 microschool located in Fredericksburg, Virginia, dedicated to supporting bright students with diverse learning needs in a small, nurturing setting where they can thrive. Our program is designed for families who are currently homeschooling or seeking a more personalized educational path—one that fosters confidence, curiosity, and a renewed love for learning. Our model has successfully helped students improve by two or more grades in one academic year!

WHY CHOOSE US

Self-paced learning to enable mastery of concepts

Learning coaches to provide small group and 1:1 support for each child

Flexible enrollment options - attend 2 or 3 days a week

APPLY TODAY!

Follow us on Facebook and Instagram @iaomaiacademy

CONTACT US

Visit: www.iaomaiacademy.com
Email: info@iaomaiacademy.com
Call: (540) 227-3904
Fredericksburg, VA 22408

SHOP NOW

GRAB YOUR COPY NOW

EmpowerHER: Narratives Rooted in Truth, Driven by Resilience, and Led by Women is a raw and powerful collection of real stories from women who've faced life's deepest hardships—and found strength on the other side. From illness and loss to trauma and recovery, these honest journeys reveal the power of resilience, healing, and inner transformation. More than survival, these stories show what it means to rise with purpose and lead with truth. You are not alone—and these women prove that even in the darkest moments, there is always a way forward, and always a reason to keep rising.

amazon.com   SHE RISES STUDIOS

FROM HOLLYWOOD SPOTLIGHT TO HOLY SURRENDER:

Ali Levine's Journey into Faith, Identity, and Divine Purpose

For years, Ali Levine was known for her glamorous appearances on red carpets, her celebrated fashion sense, and her presence in the Hollywood spotlight. A sought-after celebrity stylist and TV personality, she built a public image that sparkled with success. But behind the glitz, Ali harbored a growing emptiness that success couldn't soothe. She was chasing validation from the world, including media attention, industry praise, and a lifestyle that demanded she always be *"on."* Yet no matter how high she climbed, it was never enough to fill the gnawing void within her soul.

From the outside looking in, Ali's life seemed picture-perfect. But internally, she was crumbling. Her anxiety was mounting, burnout was consuming her, and deep disconnection weighed heavily on her spirit. Through all of this, God had been gently whispering to her heart, patiently calling her to return home. It wasn't until she hit a wall mentally, emotionally, and spiritually that she finally stopped running. She didn't just walk away from the spotlight. She turned fully toward the light of Christ.

"Surrendering was the most powerful thing I ever did," Ali shares. *"I realized my identity was never meant to be built on fame, achievement, or approval. It was always meant to be found in Him."* In that radical act of surrender, she began a new chapter. This time, it wasn't one scripted by Hollywood but one written by the hand of God.

A major turning point in her spiritual awakening came during one of the most vulnerable moments of her life: childbirth. The experience was traumatic, both physically and emotionally. It left Ali feeling shattered. But in the depths of her pain and unraveling, something miraculous happened. She encountered God more intimately than ever before. Her trauma became the doorway to transformation.

"That birth cracked me open," Ali recalls. *"I was undone in every way. But in that space of total surrender, I heard God's voice, felt His presence, and began to heal. What felt like the end became a divine rebirth. It wasn't just my daughter's birth. It was the rebirth of my spirit and purpose."*

It was in this season that Ali truly began to understand the strength that is born from surrender. The world had taught her that being strong meant pushing harder, achieving more, and hiding pain behind poise. But God showed her another way. *"He revealed to me that surrender isn't weakness.*

It's the beginning of His strength," she explains. *"It's where He meets us and restores us."*

Out of this healing process emerged a calling. It is a calling that now fuels Ali's work and ministry. She began guiding women into what she calls *"breathing with God,"* a sacred practice that goes far beyond simple breathwork. It is an embodied spiritual experience that reconnects women with the breath of life, the Holy Spirit, through Scripture, stillness, and prophetic prayer.

"To breathe with God is to inhale truth and exhale lies," Ali explains. *"It's more than calming the body. It's awakening the spirit. When we breathe with Him, we meet the Prince of Peace in a tangible, restorative way. We remember who we are and whose we are."*

Ali now leads women through Holy Spirit-led breath activations that create space for healing, clarity, and deep spiritual encounter. These moments become lifelines for women who feel overwhelmed by the pace and pressures of modern life. Women who, like Ali once did, feel lost in a whirlwind of expectations, comparison, and exhaustion.

Through her work, Ali has become a vessel of hope, especially for those who feel too far gone, too broken, or too behind in life. Her message is clear, compassionate, and grounded in God's grace. *"You are not too far gone. You are not too broken. You are not behind. God sees you, and He is right there with you, even in the chaos."*

To the woman who is weary, striving, or searching for her purpose, Ali offers this truth. Healing is an invitation, not a burden. *"You were never meant to carry it all alone,"* she says. *"Lay it at His feet. Say 'yes' to the One who already knows you, loves you, and has a plan for you."*

Ali's understanding of identity has undergone a total transformation since her journey into faith. She no longer defines herself by what she achieves or how she's perceived. Instead, she stands firm in the truth that she is chosen, loved, redeemed, and seen, not by the world, but by God.

"Before Christ, my identity was all over the place. It was shaped by the roles I played, the applause I chased, and the image I curated," she says. *"Now, I know I'm not what I do. I'm whose I am. That truth has changed everything."*

This identity shift has deeply impacted every part of her life. It affects how she mothers her children, how she leads others, how she speaks, and how she shows up in the world. No longer living from hustle, she now lives from a place of rest. Her worth is no longer measured in likes, followers, or accolades. It is rooted in eternity.

As she reflects on her journey, Ali acknowledges the cost of walking away from the spotlight. But she also recognizes the immeasurable gain of stepping into a life led by the Spirit. *"I gave it all to Him, my career, my pain, my plans, and I took the biggest trust fall of my life. And He caught me."*

Ali's story is not just one of redemption. It is a reminder that God uses every part of our story, even the painful chapters,

to draw us closer to Him and reveal our true purpose. Through her life, Ali invites others to do the same. Stop striving. Start surrendering. Let God breathe new life into your heart.

Because in the end, it's not about the spotlight. It's about the Light.

Connect With Ali

www.alilevine.com

AMBER KRYSTAL:

A Voice for Healing, Wholeness and Maturity

Amber Krystal is a dynamic faith leader, speaker, and spiritual mentor known for her bold message of healing, wholeness, and maturity. As the founder of HWMM Ministries and the visionary behind Be Healed. Be Whole. Be Mature: A Place of Metamorphosis, Amber has committed her life to guiding people through the life-changing journey of personal and spiritual transformation.

Affectionately called The Female Moses, Amber walks in a prophetic mandate to lead others out of the bondage of past trauma, fear, and religious legalism into a life of authentic freedom and divine purpose. Her ministry was birthed from a deeply personal wilderness season, where God revealed to her the necessity of inner healing before destiny could be fulfilled. Amber teaches that true confidence, leadership, and influence are rooted in transparency, spiritual maturity, and a healed heart.

Her bold, unfiltered message has opened doors across both ministry and marketplace platforms. Amber has been featured in AP News, Yahoo Global Media, Google News, Paramount films, and Hallmark movies and holds an IMDb credit for her work in the entertainment industry. A published writer and rising media personality, she recently graced the cover of Neuworldz Magazine, a digital magazine with over 1M viewers, sharing her heart for women navigating transformation and healing.

Amber's powerful voice reached global audiences when she took the TEDx stage, boldly declaring the importance of confronting brokenness to access destiny. Her talk, much like her ministry, challenged conventional mindsets and inspired a movement of people determined to embrace their metamorphosis.

Her latest book, A Call to the Wilderness: A Pursuit to Purpose and Destiny, captures the prophetic insight and hard-earned wisdom gleaned from her own spiritual journey. In it, Amber shares how seasons of isolation and pruning are often divine setups for extraordinary purpose.

Through her syndicated podcast, speaking engagements, and growing online ministry, Amber Krystal continues to lead a new generation of believers toward healing, identity, and bold spiritual maturity. Her life and message serve as a reminder that transformation isn't a suggestion — it's a requirement for those destined to impact the world.

Connect With Amber

www.hwmministries.com
Instagram: @iamamberkrystal
Facebook: Amber Krystal

THIS IS JUST THE BEGINNING OF SOMETHING BIG!

By Kaila Nike

Losing my job was the turning point; that's when I truly committed to entrepreneurship.

I've always had an entrepreneurial spirit, but as a single mom and sole provider, stability was always my priority. The 9-to-5 offered that steady paycheck, which was a sure thing. Still, for years, I actively sought an exit, trying to find a way to escape the corporate world. Nothing ever stuck, though. It felt forced, like I was desperate to work for myself and just grasping at any opportunity. I'd jump from one idea to the next, only to end up in the same frustrating cycle. I realize now that it was because I wasn't aligned with those ventures. Unknowingly, I was ignoring a deep, burning desire within me. I wasn't purposefully shutting it out, but I was so focused on making other things *"work"* that I simply wasn't listening to myself.

As time went on, that inner desire grew louder: I wanted to write. I'd carried stories within me for so long, and they were desperate to be told. So, when I received a ten-day notice that I was going to be losing my job, I knew I was ready. I welcomed it because I knew it was time to listen to that nagging desire that lived inside of me for so long. I truly believe the universe heard my longing and created the space for me to finally pursue my dream of becoming a full-time, published author.

From that moment on, I went all in without a single hesitation. I immediately began developing a story that had been pressing on my mind for years into a series called Mystique. To all romantasy fans, I truly encourage you to check it out. Was it easy? The writing itself flowed, even though I once thought that was the hardest part. The real challenge came with the steep learning curve of the publishing world, understanding editing, and mastering the intricacies of writing a professional novel. But after countless hours, I made it happen.

Over a year has passed since I lost my job, and I've immersed myself daily in writing and learning. This is clearly my true path; it feels right, aligned, and just naturally easy (in the sense that I enjoy it), as if it was always meant to be. Beyond my romantasy series, I'm also delving into numerous other projects, from exploring the fantasy realm to contributing to several personal growth anthologies. Each of these is either already out or set to be released this year or next. With some work already available and much more in the pipeline, I've already earned national and international best-seller status. I never dreamed it would happen so quickly, but here I am. If I can achieve this, you can too.

My journey has barely begun. I have a much broader vision: to inspire and support others who are on a similar path, helping them align with their own dreams. This is precisely why I also choose to write about personal growth. I've gained so much from my own journey and years of trial and error; if I can help fast-track someone else's success, that would be a dream fulfilled. Inspiring just one person to take that leap of faith and start creating their dream life would make every step of my own experience worthwhile.

If I could offer one piece of advice to aspiring authors right now, it would be this: honor your desire. Tune into that profound voice within, and simply take the leap of faith. When your deepest longing aligns with your vision, you'll find that everything begins to click into place. Unseen opportunities will surface, and new doors will open. The key, however, is to take inspired action—action that resonates deeply with your desires. From there, commit fully and never look back. Your stories are needed; there are people out there eager to read them. This saying always comes to mind: *"The best time to start was ten years ago; the next best time is now."* So, what are you waiting for?

For exclusive offers, and to check out my current projects, scan the QR code below or visit my website at *www.kailanike.com*

Connect With Kaila

www.tiktok.com/@kailanikeauthor
www.facebook.com/kaila.em.9
www.facebook.com/profile.php?
id=61564802221645
www.instagram.com/kailanike.author

SHE RISES
STUDIOS

*U*NLEASH YOUR STORY
BECOME A PUBLISHED AUTHOR!

Have you ever dreamed of sharing your wisdom, experience, or passion with the world? **Now is your time!**

Publishing a book isn't just about writing—it's about **establishing your authority, inspiring others, and creating a lasting legac**y. Plus, with the **$138.5 billion book industry** booming, there's never been a better moment to step into the spotlight.

At **SRS Publishing**, we don't just publish books—we **elevate voices, empower authors, and create change-makers**. Our mission is to help women break barriers, amplify their stories, and thrive in the publishing world. Whether you're an entrepreneur, thought leader, or storyteller at heart, **we're here to guide you every step of the way.**

JOIN THE FASTEST-GROWING PUBLISHING HOUSE FOR WOMEN IN THE USA.

READY TO TURN YOUR DREAM INTO REALITY?

 www.SheRisesStudios.com | contact@sherisesstudios.com

GET YOUR COPY NOW

Celebrate the power of women through inspiring stories and insights.

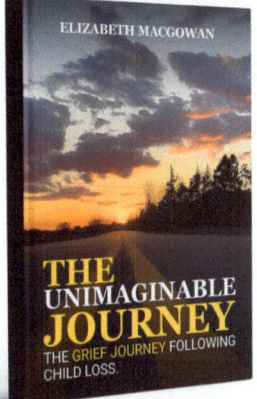

The Unimaginable Journey
Beth MacGowan

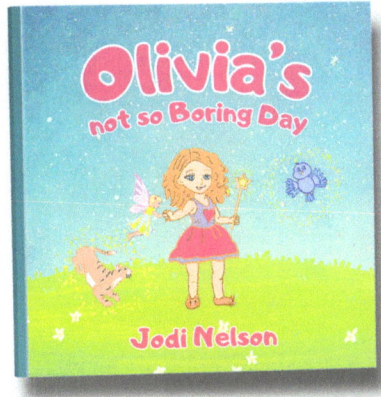

Olivia's Not So Boring Day
Jodi Nelson

Cosmic Butterflies
Tymquana Frierson

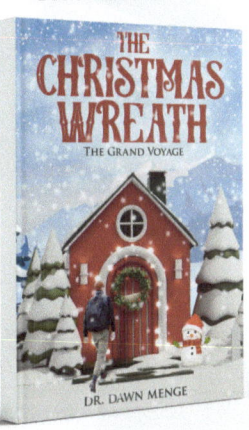

The Christmas Wreath
Dr.Dawn Menge

Dreaming with My Eyes Open
Michela Perry

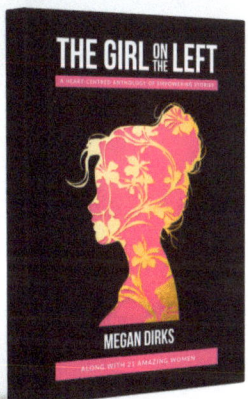

The Girl on the Left
Megan Dirks

A Certain Kind of Sadness
Jillean McClory

Cruz Control
Melissa Cruz

Retreat Within Me
Hoda Jaludi

www.ingramcontent.com/pod-product-compliance
Lightning Source LLC
Chambersburg PA
CBHW041430120626
46547CB00002B/160